D0579882

SCARY PLACES

Shuttered
Horror Hospitals

by Dinah Williams

Consultant: Troy Taylor
President of the American Ghost Society

BEARPORT
PUBLISHING

New York, New York

Credits

Cover and Title Page, © Andrea Gingerich/iStockphoto and © Suzanne Tucker/Shutterstock; 4–5, © Alice Marie Photography; 6, © Graham Toney/Alamy; 7, © Stephen Mulcahey/Alamy; 8, © Ted Lum; 9L, © CB2/ZOB/WENN/Newscom; 9R, © Ransom Riggs; 10, © Daniel Hellerman; 11, © Alice Marie Photography; 12, © Hawaiian Legacy Archive/Pacific Stock/Photolibrary; 13, © C. Walker/Topham/ The Image Works; 14, © Dr. Mangor; 15L, © Dr. Mangor; 15R, © Ty Supancic; 16, Courtesy of Hauntedchangi.com; 17, © Lu Yee; 18, © Christopher Payne Photography; 19T, Courtesy of The New York Public Library; 19B, © Mary Evans Picture Library/The Image Works; 20, © Shenandoah Valley Paranormal Society; 21L, © Shenandoah Valley Paranormal Society; 21R, © ULPA 1994.18.0758/ Herald-Post Collection/Special Collections/University of Louisville Photographic Archives; 22, © Stock Montage/SuperStock; 23L, Courtesy of Gettysburgdaily.com; 23R, Medical kit of Doctor Henry Caperton (wood & metal), American School, (19th century)/Museum of the Confederacy, Richmond, Virginia, USA/Civil War Archive/The Bridgeman Art Library International; 24, Courtesy of The Verona Public Library; 25T, © B. Speckart/Shutterstock; 25B, © Rusty Tagliareni; 26B, © LBDV Design Services; 26T, © LBDV Design Services; 27, © LBDV Design Services; 31, © JirkaBursik/Shutterstock.

Publisher: Kenn Goin
Editorial Director: Adam Siegel
Creative Director: Spencer Brinker
Design: Dawn Beard Creative
Cover: Kim Jones
Photo Researcher: Picture Perfect Professionals, LLC

Library of Congress Cataloging-in-Publication Data

Williams, Dinah.
  Shuttered horror hospitals / by Dinah Williams.
    p. cm. — (Scary places)
  Includes bibliographical references (p.   ) and index.
  ISBN-13: 978-1-61772-148-9 (library binding)
  ISBN-10: 1-61772-148-4 (library binding)
  1. Haunted hospitals—Juvenile literature. I. Title.
  BF1474.4.W55 2011
  133.1'22—dc22
                        2010034522

For more information, write to Bearport Publishing Company, Inc., 101 Fifth Avenue, Suite 6R, New York, New York 10003. Printed in the United States of America in North Mankato, Minnesota.

122010
10810CGD

10 9 8 7 6 5 4 3 2 1

Contents

Shuttered Horror Hospitals. 4

New Hospital, Old Ghost. 6

Island of Death 8

Abused and Abandoned. 10

Left to Die. 12

Horror Movie Hospital 14

World War II Ghosts 16

The Trail of Typhoid Mary. 18

Fresh Air, Sunshine, and Death. 20

The Battle to Live 22

Spirits at the Sanatorium 24

A Haunted Hospital 26

Shuttered Horror Hospitals Around the World 28

Glossary 30

Bibliography 31

Read More. 31

Learn More Online. 31

Index. 32

About the Author. 32

Shuttered Horror Hospitals

Hospitals are places where sick or injured people go to become well. Doctors and nurses use the most up-to-date treatments to help heal everything from small cuts and bruises to serious illnesses and diseases.

In the past, however, it was very hard for doctors to help their patients. They often didn't have the medicines and tools that were needed to save people's lives. They also didn't always understand what was causing their patients' illnesses. As a result, people in hospitals often didn't get better—and many of them died.

Pennhurst State School and Hospital in Spring City, Pennsylvania

While most of the hospitals in this book have all been shut down or abandoned, many say that their sad and sometimes terrifying histories live on. Among these hospitals, you'll discover a huge medical facility abandoned by everyone but the ghosts of long-dead patients, a hospital that is so creepy it is used as a movie set for horror films, and a temporary hospital built on a battlefield that is now considered one of the most haunted spots in America.

New Hospital, Old Ghost

Royal Derby Hospital, Derby, England

Hundreds of millions of dollars were spent to build a shiny new hospital in Derby, England. When the hospital was completed in 2009, patients expected to receive the finest medical care. What they didn't expect, however, was a 2,000-year-old ghost.

Royal Derby Hospital

Derby has one of the longest and most haunted histories of all the cities in England. In fact, people report seeing so many ghosts in Derby that it is known as the ghost capital of the country.

The city was originally built on the site of a Roman **fort** that dates back to 80 A.D. The new hospital was constructed over one of the ancient Roman roads that once ran through Derby. Some say that recent work on the hospital disturbed the place where a Roman soldier died thousands of years ago. Does the ghost of that soldier now haunt the hospital's halls?

Several hospital workers claim to have seen a ghostly male figure dressed in a black **cloak**. He darts between rooms and walks through walls. Many say that he is often spotted near the hospital's **morgue**. Employees are so afraid that those in charge are trying to find a way to frighten the ghost away.

A Roman soldier dressed for battle

Lionel Fanthorpe, an expert on the **paranormal**, has found 315 reports of ghosts, werewolves, and vampires in Derby since records were first kept.

Island of Death

Poveglia Mental Hospital, Poveglia, Italy

Hundreds of years ago, Venice, Italy, was a major trading center. Thousands of ships passed through its **port**. While some brought treasures, others brought death and disease. Could a nearby island, such as Poveglia, help save the people of Venice?

A horrible disease called **plague** hit Venice in 1576. This disease spreads quickly from person to person. When plague attacks someone, it causes fever, bleeding under the skin, coughing up blood, and, often within a few days, death. During an **outbreak** in the 1500s, nearly a third of the people in Venice died.

The island of Poveglia

Terrified, people looked for a way to stop the illness from spreading. One solution was to force victims who might pass on the disease to live on nearby islands, including Poveglia. It didn't take long, however, for the dead in these places to quickly outnumber the living. As the victims of plague died, their **corpses** were shoveled into huge **grave** pits. As many as 160,000 are said to have died on the island of Poveglia.

In 1922, a **mental hospital** was built on the island. According to reports, ghosts of plague victims haunted the mentally ill—and the hospital's director. Even worse, the director was said to have performed cruel experiments on his patients in order to try to cure them. He eventually went mad and threw himself off the top of the island's church. According to **legend**, he survived the fall, only to be **strangled** by a ghostly mist when he reached the ground.

Inside Poveglia's abandoned mental hospital

A woman's skull from the 1500s with a brick stuck between its jaws

During the 1500s, some people believed that plague victims became vampires. To stop them from attacking people and drinking their blood, gravediggers shoved a stone or brick into the mouths of corpses that they believed had become vampires. They hoped this would cause them to starve to death.

Abused and Abandoned

Pennhurst State School and Hospital, Spring City, Pennsylvania

In 1908, Pennhurst State School and Hospital opened to help care for people with mental and physical **disabilities**. Unfortunately, the hospital did not have enough money or workers to help the thousands of patients crowded into the building. More than a few died. According to some, a handful of their ghosts still haunt this horror hospital that was their home.

Pennhurst State School and Hospital

In 1946, there were only seven doctors serving more than 2,000 patients at Pennhurst State School and Hospital. By 1955, there were about 3,500 patients. Because there were so few people on staff, many patients were forced to spend their days and nights locked in metal cribs. That way, they would stay in one place. Others wandered around naked because no one would help them get dressed.

When the staff tried to control patients, they sometimes went too far. Patients' bones were broken and teeth were knocked out by those who were supposed to care for them. To stop the mistreatment, the hospital was closed in 1987.

Pennhurst has had such a sad and disturbing history, how could the **spirits** of troubled patients not **linger** there? People who have visited the abandoned hospital say that they have heard voices in the narrow, dark tunnels that connect the buildings. Others have heard screams and slamming doors. Even those who haven't heard anything still have the uneasy feeling of being watched.

Inside the abandoned hospital

Terri Lee Halderman was 12 years old when she was admitted to Pennhurst. During the 11 years she was there, her medical records reported more than 40 injuries. These included the loss of several teeth, broken fingers and toes, and numerous cuts, scratches, and bites. Her lawsuit in 1974 was one reason the hospital was finally closed.

Left to Die

Leper Colony on the Island of Molokai, Hawaii

Leprosy is a disease that attacks a person's nerves, skin, and eyes. Before a cure was found, many people who had leprosy were **quarantined** so that they couldn't spread the disease to others. One place they were sent was to the island of Molokai (*mah*-luh-KYE), Hawaii. Few who were forced to live there ever left.

On January 6, 1866, a dozen people who were suffering from leprosy were dropped off on the rocky island of Molokai, Hawaii. To survive, they were given only a few shovels and axes, wool blankets, some beef, bread, and two cottages to live in. Each week ships brought more victims of the disease.

Molokai island

For years, doctors at the small hospital on the island could do nothing more to help their patients than change their bandages. When examining the wounds of a leper, one doctor used his cane—rather than his hand—to lift up the victim's bandages. He was afraid that if he touched his patient he would soon catch the disease himself.

Leprosy victims from countries around the world, including the United States, China, Spain, England, France, Korea, and Japan, were sent to Molokai. Between 1866 and 1969, more than 8,000 victims were torn from their families and forced to live on the island. About half were between the ages of 11 and 25.

The graves of people on Molokai who died from leprosy

Leprosy begins with a rash that slowly spreads over a person's body. The disease causes victims to lose feeling in their skin. Fingers and toes may curl up as hands and feet become weak. Some sufferers even go blind. Today, there are medicines to cure leprosy.

Horror Movie Hospital

Linda Vista Hospital, Los Angeles, California

This hospital in Los Angeles, California, was once one of the best in the country. Today, some people say Linda Vista is now one of the best places to find ghosts.

The Linda Vista Hospital was first established in 1904 for railroad employees. Workers who had diseases such as **tuberculosis** or who were injured on the job got first-class treatment. As the years passed, however, a hospital that was prized for its excellent care steadily declined.

With little money to run the hospital, the staff could no longer provide care to the sick as well as all the victims of gun shot wounds and stabbings that came through its doors. In 1991, the last patient checked out of Linda Vista, and the hospital was shut down.

Since then, ghost hunters have found many spirits in the building. Some of them claim to have heard a little girl crying for help from the fifth floor. Others have seen a doctor who roams the corridors. There is also a strange green light that appears at night from some of the windows.

The hospital is now so frightening that it has been the setting for a number of horror movies. One film crew member said, "Everything is fine in most of the building, but there are places where the air suddenly changes. There's a feeling that if I go any further, if I keep walking in that direction, something's going to get me."

Inside the abandoned hospital

According to some, the ghosts at Linda Vista smash locks, break windows, and knock down doors.

World War II Ghosts

Old Changi Hospital, Changi Village, Singapore

Down the dark narrow streets of Changi (CHANG-ee) Village lies the abandoned Old Changi Hospital. Once a military hospital, it is now considered by some to be the most haunted spot in one of Asia's most ghost-filled cities.

Old Changi Hospital

During World War II (1939–1945), the Japanese invaded the island of Singapore. During the three years they controlled the country, from 1942 to 1945, the Japanese were cruel to its citizens. They killed as many as 50,000 people who were thought to be anti-Japanese. More than 7,000 prisoners of war were crammed into the small prison in Changi Village.

In the 1930s, a hospital had been built in Changi. During the Japanese invasion in 1942, however, it was turned into a place of great suffering. The Japanese secret police were said to have set up a torture chamber in the building. They used pain to get information from prisoners about their country's war plans.

In 1997, the Old Changi Hospital was shut down when a newer hospital was built nearby. According to some, however, reminders of the hospital's painful past remain. The ghosts of the victims of the Japanese are sometimes spotted at the abandoned hospital—often missing their heads and feet.

Inside Old Changi Hospital

In 2010, a film crew visited Old Changi Hospital. They hoped to prove that the abandoned building was haunted. It didn't take long to do so. One night soon after filming began, a terrifying ghost-like figure was said to have appeared. The crew ran out of the hospital in fear.

The Trail of Typhoid Mary

Riverside Hospital, North Brother Island, New York

Although millions of people live in New York City today, no one makes a home on the city's North Brother Island. Yet for more than 75 years, the island's hospital was a place where many people came to stay—until they died.

Riverside Hospital's tuberculosis building

In 1885, Riverside Hospital was opened to care for victims of deadly diseases including smallpox, **typhus**, and tuberculosis. During the 1892 typhus outbreak, New Yorkers who showed **symptoms** were immediately put on a ferry and sent to the hospital. Many never returned. About 1,200 people were quarantined at Riverside to try and stop the spread of the disease.

Over the years, the most famous of all the patients at Riverside was Mary Mallon, a cook better known as Typhoid Mary. Although she had **typhoid fever**, she didn't feel sick. As a result, Mary didn't believe she was spreading the disease and refused to stop working. During her lifetime, Mary is known to have infected at least 47 people. In the early 1900s, health authorities finally tracked her down and forced her to stay at Riverside Hospital. She spent 26 years there, until her death in 1938.

Mary Mallon

In 1904, an overcrowded ferry called the *General Slocum* burst into flames in New York's East River. With rotted life jackets and useless lifeboats, it ran aground on North Brother Island. Nurses and doctors from Riverside Hospital rushed into the water to help. Still, more than 1,000 people died.

Illustration of the
General Slocum disaster

Fresh Air, Sunshine, and Death

Waverly Hills Sanatorium, Louisville, Kentucky

Tuberculosis is a terrifying illness that attacks a person's lungs. People who suffer from the deadly disease have chest pain and trouble breathing, and they may even cough up blood. Before effective medicines were developed in the 1940s, many victims hoped that special tuberculosis hospitals called **sanatoriums** would save them. Sadly, many of those people ended up dead.

Waverly Hills Sanatorium

Waverly Hills was a huge sanatorium built on a hill in Louisville, Kentucky. The hospital opened in 1926. Tuberculosis patients who stayed there hoped that the fresh air, sunshine, and rest that Waverly Hills provided would save them. Unfortunately for most, it didn't. Before the tuberculosis hospital closed in 1961, around 6,000 patients are believed to have died there.

When the disease was at its worst, someone died nearly every day at Waverly Hills. Those who worked at the hospital needed a way to transport the dead bodies without upsetting the patients who were trying to get well. So they used rail cars that secretly traveled down a tunnel 500 feet (152 m) long from the hospital to **hearses** waiting below. The pitch-black tunnel soon became known as the body chute.

The body chute at Waverly Hills

When so many people die in one place, some believe their spirits are bound to remain. Stories say that in 1928, the head nurse in Room 502 killed herself. Her sad spirit is thought by some to still haunt the empty building.

Patients resting at Waverly Hills

The Battle to Live

Camp Letterman General Hospital, Gettysburg, Pennsylvania

One of the bloodiest battles in history was fought during the U.S. Civil War (1861–1865). For three days in July 1863, more than 150,000 soldiers clashed in Gettysburg, Pennsylvania, with around 50,000 killed, wounded, or missing. For many of these injured soldiers, Camp Letterman General Hospital was just a brief stop on their way to the graveyard.

The Battle of Gettysburg

Following the horror of the Battle of Gettysburg, thousands of wounded soldiers were sent by trains to hospitals. However, nearly 5,000 soldiers were too badly injured to be moved. To help care for them, a hospital called Camp Letterman was set up on the battlefield on July 22, 1863.

Five hundred tents were filled with the sick and wounded. According to one nurse, "shrieks, cries, and groans" could be heard all around. "Not only from those in the tents," she added, "but on the **amputating tables**, which were almost constantly occupied." If the **surgery** didn't kill the soldiers, **infections** or diarrhea often did. Ghosts of the many soldiers who failed to survive have been spotted on the battlefield. One, a young, legless man, appears to guests at a motel that was built over a site of heavy fighting. Today, Gettysburg is considered one of the most haunted places in America.

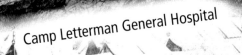

Camp Letterman General Hospital

At the time of the Civil War, medicines that could stop a wound in an arm or leg from becoming infected had not been developed yet. Instead of treating the wound, doctors often simply cut off the injured limb using saws and knives.

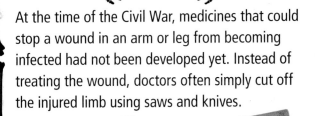

Tools used by Civil War doctors to cut off injured legs and arms

Spirits at the Sanatorium

Essex Mountain Sanatorium, Verona, New Jersey

The Essex Mountain Sanatorium claimed that 50 percent of its patients recovered from tuberculosis. Yet what happened to the other half that weren't so lucky? Some say they have never left the building.

Essex Mountain Sanatorium

In 1906, there were more than 3,000 cases of tuberculosis in the city of Newark, New Jersey. Many of the victims of the disease were sent to a former **orphanage** that eventually became the sprawling Essex Mountain Sanatorium. At the bottom of the mountain sat Overbrook, a large mental institution. As tuberculosis began to be controlled by medication in the 1940s, the sanatorium gradually emptied out and closed for good in 1977.

Abandoned for years, the Essex Mountain Sanatorium became so scary that people went there only on a dare. Escaped mental patients were said to live in the dark tunnels that ran beneath the hospital. Some visitors say they have seen an empty wheelchair move by itself. Others have heard whispers in empty rooms, as well as someone yelling "Get out!" Many visitors took that advice and ran. The horror hospital was demolished in 2002.

Some of the patients at Overbrook were as frightening as the ghosts at the abandoned sanatorium. One patient escaped in his pajamas, stole a carving knife and hammer, and tried to kidnap a woman who lived nearby. Another supposedly ate his entire bed, including the mattress and headboard.

Overbrook mental hospital

A Haunted Hospital

The Spanish Military Hospital Museum, St. Augustine, Florida

St. Augustine, Florida, was founded in 1565 by Spanish explorers. The hospital that was built there in 1784, the Royal Hospital of Our Lady of Guadalupe, was a temporary home to those injured in clashes with **Native Americans** or in wars. Some say the site is now a permanent home to many ghosts.

Spanish Military Hospital Museum

SPANISH MILITARY HOSPITAL MUSEUM

HOURS:

Monday - Saturday : 10am - 4:30pm
Sunday : Noon - 4:00 pm
Closed: Thanksgiving, Christmas Eve and Christmas Day

The Royal Hospital of Our Lady of Guadalupe was torn down in 1821. Years later, the Spanish Military Hospital Museum was built on the site to show visitors what it was like to be a patient there in 1791. The tour visits the **mourning** room, where patients were blessed by a priest moments before they died. It also shows the surgery room, where cutting off an arm or a leg was often the only way to save a life.

While visitors learn about the hospital's history, they may also meet some of the ghosts who have been haunting this building for many years. Some people who have visited the mourning room claimed the bed looked like someone was lying on it—but no one was there. According to reports from visitors, other beds have been pushed across rooms by unseen hands. The sounds of footsteps, moans, and sobbing have come from empty rooms. The many ghosts have also reportedly touched, pushed, and even bitten unsuspecting visitors.

The mourning room

In 1821, workers demolished the hospital to put in new water pipes for the city. Buried deep under the building were piles of human bones. It is now believed that the hospital was built over an old Native American burial site. Some believe this is another reason the area is so haunted.

Shuttered Horror Hospitals

Linda Vista Hospital
Los Angeles, California

A haunted hospital is now used for horror movies.

Riverside Hospital
North Brother Island, New York

This hospital for infectious diseases once housed Typhoid Mary.

Essex Mountain Sanatorium
Verona, New Jersey

Setting up a hospital next to a mental institution leads to some frightful happenings.

Pacific Ocean

NORTH AMERICA

Atlantic Ocean

Leper Colony
Molokai, Hawaii

A small hospital could do little to help thousands of leprosy victims.

Pennhurst State School and Hospital
Spring City, Pennsylvania

This hospital for people with disabilities was closed for abuse.

SOUTH AMERICA

Waverly Hills Sanatorium
Louisville, Kentucky

Fresh air and sunshine weren't enough to cure the thousands who died at this hospital.

The Spanish Military Hospital Museum
St. Augustine, Florida

This old hospital is haunted by even older spirits.

Camp Letterman General Hospital
Gettysburg, Pennsylvania

Hundreds of tents made up this temporary hospital where limbs as well as lives were lost.

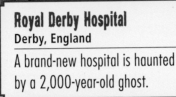

Around the World

Arctic Ocean

Royal Derby Hospital
Derby, England

A brand-new hospital is haunted by a 2,000-year-old ghost.

EUROPE

ASIA

Poveglia Mental Hospital
Poveglia, Italy

An abandoned mental hospital sits on an island where thousands of plague victims are buried.

AFRICA

Indian Ocean

Old Changi Hospital
Changi Village, Singapore

Spirits from World War II haunt this abandoned hospital.

AUSTRALIA

Southern Ocean

ANTARCTICA

Glossary

amputating tables (AM-pyoo-*tayt*-ing TAY-buhlz) tables on which an arm or a leg is cut off for medical reasons

cloak (KLOHK) a loose coat with no sleeves that is often worn to hide someone

corpses (KORPS-iz) dead bodies

disabilities (*diss*-uh-BIL-uh-teez) conditions that make it hard for people to do everyday things, such as walking, seeing, or hearing

fort (FORT) a strong building from which people can defend an area

grave (GRAYV) a hole dug into the ground where a dead person is buried

hearses (HURSS-iz) cars that carry coffins to be buried

infections (in-FEK-shuhnz) illnesses caused by germs entering the body

legend (LEJ-uhnd) a story that is handed down from the past that may be based on fact but is not always completely true

linger (LING-ur) to remain longer than expected

mental hospital (MEN-tuhl HOSS-pit-uhl) a medical facility that takes care of people whose minds aren't working properly

morgue (MORG) a place where dead bodies are kept before being buried

mourning (MORN-ing) feeling very sad for someone who has died

Native Americans (NAY-tiv uh-MER-uh-kinz) the first people to live in America; they are sometimes called American Indians

orphanage (OR-fuh-nij) a place where orphans—children whose parents are dead—live and are cared for

outbreak (OUT-*brayk*) a sudden start or increase in the activity of something, such as the spread of a disease

paranormal (*pa*-ruh-NOR-muhl) events that are not able to be scientifically explained

plague (PLAYG) a deadly disease that is spread by fleas and rodents

port (PORT) a place where ships load and unload goods

quarantined (KWOR-uhn-*teend*) separated from other people in order to prevent the spread of a disease

sanatoriums (*san*-uh-TOR-ee-uhmz) buildings where patients suffering from certain long-term diseases stay to increase their health and ease symptoms

spirits (SPIHR-its) supernatural creatures, such as ghosts

strangled (STRANG-uhld) choked to death

surgery (SUR-jur-ee) the part of medical science that treats injuries or diseases by fixing or removing parts of the body

symptoms (SIMP-tuhmz) signs of a disease or other physical problem felt by a person

tuberculosis (too-*bur*-kyuh-LOH-siss) a disease that usually affects the lungs and causes fever, coughing, and difficulty breathing

typhoid fever (TYE-foyd FEE-vur) a disease spread by bacteria that cause fever, diarrhea, weakness, and headaches

typhus (TYE-fuhss) any one of a group of diseases spread by fleas, lice, and mites that cause fever and weakness

Bibliography

Belanger, Jeff. *The World's Most Haunted Places: From the Secret Files of Ghostvillage.com.* New York: Sterling (2007).

Coulombe, Charles A. *Haunted Places in America: A Guide to Spooked and Spooky Public Places in the United States.* Guilford, CT: The Lyons Press (2004).

Hauck, Dennis William. *Haunted Places: The National Directory.* New York: Penguin Books (2002).

Read More

Guy, John A. *Ghosts.* Costa Mesa, CA: Saddleback (2010).

Hamilton, John. *Haunted Places.* Edina, MN: ABDO Publishing Company (2007).

Hawes, Jason, and Grant Wilson. *Ghost Hunt: Chilling Tales of the Unknown.* New York: Little, Brown and Company (2010).

Williams, Dinah. *Abandoned Insane Asylums (Scary Places).* New York: Bearport (2008).

Learn More Online

To learn more about shuttered horror hospitals, visit
www.bearportpublishing.com/ScaryPlaces

Index

Camp Letterman General
  Hospital 22–23, 28
Changi Village, Singapore 16–17,
  29

Derby, England 6–7, 29

Essex Mountain Sanatorium
  24–25, 28

General Slocum 19
Gettysburg, Pennsylvania 22–23,
  28

leprosy 12–13, 28
Linda Vista Hospital 14–15, 28
Los Angeles, California 14–15, 28
Louisville, Kentucky 20–21, 28

Mallon, Mary 19
Molokai, Hawaii 12–13, 28

North Brother Island, New York
  18–19, 28

Old Changi Hospital 16–17, 29
Overbrook 25

Pennhurst State School and
  Hospital 4, 10–11, 28
plague 8–9, 29
Poveglia, Italy, 8–9, 29
Poveglia Mental Hospital 8–9, 29

Riverside Hospital 18–19, 28
Royal Derby Hospital 6–7, 29

Spanish Military Hospital
  Museum 26–27, 28
Spring City, Pennsylvania 4,
  10–11, 28
St. Augustine, Florida 26–27, 28

tuberculosis 14, 18–19, 20–21,
  24–25
Typhoid Mary 18–19, 28
typhus 19

U.S. Civil War 22–23

Venice, Italy 8
Verona, New Jersey 24–25, 28

Waverly Hills Sanatorium 20–21,
  28
World War II 17, 29

About the Author

Dinah Williams is an editor and children's book author. Her books include *Shocking Seafood*; *Slithery, Slimy, Scaly Treats*; *Abandoned Insane Asylums*; *Haunted Houses*; and *Spooky Cemeteries*, which won the 2009 Children's Choice Book Award. She lives in Cranford, New Jersey.